How to play

AMERICAN FOOTBALL

a step-by-step guide

Text:
Liz French

Technical consultant:
Wayne Persinger
Chairman
Norwich American Football Club

JARROLD

Other titles in this series are:

BADMINTON	**DINGHY SAILING**	**SQUASH**
BASKETBALL	**GET FIT FOR SPORT**	**SWIMMING**
BOWLS	**GOLF**	**TABLE TENNIS**
COARSE FISHING	**HOCKEY**	**TENNIS**
CRICKET	**SNOOKER**	**WINDSURFING**
CROQUET	**SOCCER**	

How to play AMERICAN FOOTBALL
ISBN 0-7117-0514-3
First published in Great Britain, 1991
Text copyright © Liz French, 1991
This edition copyright © 1991 Jarrold Publishing
Illustrations by Ryz Hajdul

Designed and produced by
Parke Sutton Limited, Norwich
for Jarrold Publishing, Norwich

Contents

Introduction

American football is undoubtedly a dramatic success story in the UK. It has become the fastest-growing participatory sport, as well as compulsive viewing for the millions of fans who enjoy its television coverage.

This book aims to give a clear explanation of the game, as well as guidance on techniques and tactics and plenty of hints for effective practice. Because the terminology of the game can be confusing at first, unfamiliar words and phrases are printed in italics as they appear in the book and are defined in the glossary on pages 47-48.

American football is exciting to watch and challenging to play; it requires strength, agility and courage as well as skill — and so much happens so fast during a game that seven officials are needed to oversee the action!

Despite its apparent complexity, American football is actually based on quite simple principles.

The game was developed in the 1870s as an American version of rugby, and today the two games still bear a superficial resemblance.

The ball and the goal posts are similar, and in both games the players aim to make forward progress with the ball and earn points both by getting the ball over the goal line and by scoring goals. However, American football is a more complex game, more dependent on finely planned tactics, formations and strategies. Players adopt highly specialised roles, and with unlimited substitutions allowed, whole units with special functions can be brought into and out of play according to the requirements of any situation.

Of course, no book can replace good coaching, and if you are serious about the game, you will want to join a club. There are over 150 senior and 100 junior teams in Britain, and you can contact the British American Football Association (BAFA) at 92 Palace Garden Terrace, London W8 4RS for details of clubs in your area.

Note: The rules and pitch markings for college (*NCAA*) football are slightly different from those of the professional (*NFL*) game. This book refers to the *NFL* rules, which correspond most closely to those used in the UK game. A full set of rules can be obtained from the BAFA, address above.

FIELD AND EQUIPMENT

The Field

The game is played on a grass or an artificial surface 360 ft long and 160 ft wide, with numbered white lines marked every ten yds across its width as shown here. The grid pattern created by the pitch markings has inspired the name Gridiron by which the pitch is commonly known.

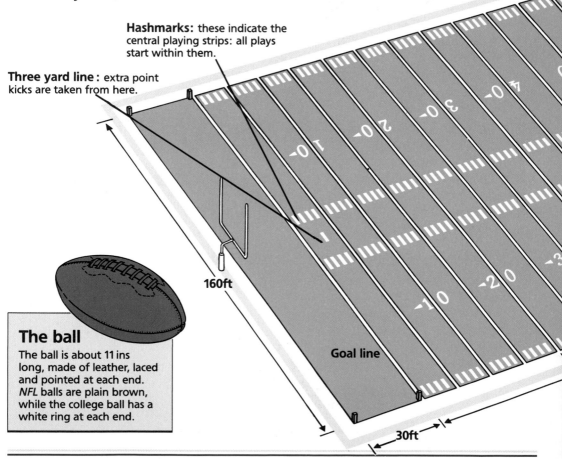

Hashmarks: these indicate the central playing strips: all plays start within them.

Three yard line: extra point kicks are taken from here.

160ft

Goal line

30ft

The ball

The ball is about 11 ins long, made of leather, laced and pointed at each end. *NFL* balls are plain brown, while the college ball has a white ring at each end.

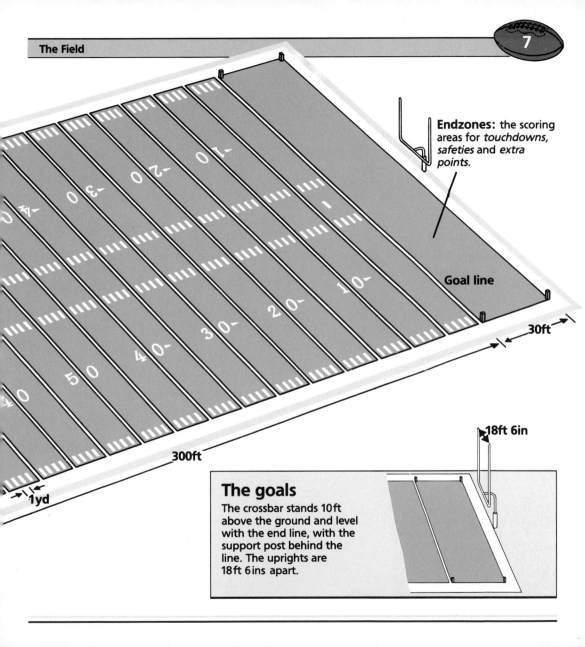

Endzones: the scoring areas for *touchdowns*, *safeties* and *extra points.*

Goal line

30ft

300ft

1yd

18ft 6in

The goals

The crossbar stands 10ft above the ground and level with the end line, with the support post behind the line. The uprights are 18ft 6ins apart.

Players' Equipment

American football is a tough game and protective equipment is vital for all players, even if it does make you feel like a knight in armour! The items labelled (C) in this diagram are compulsory under the British rules; those marked (O) are optional. The protection needed will vary according to your playing position and personal preference.

Helmet (C): with built-in face mask and chin strap, usually printed with team colours and logo.

Gum shield (C): this is attached to the face guards.

Collar (O)

Arm pad (O)

Chest and shoulder pads (C)

Rib protector (O)

Elbow pad (O)

Spine pad (C)

Hip pad (C)

Gloves (O): players can wrap tape around their fingers to help them catch the ball instead of wearing gloves.

Thigh pad (C): these fit in pockets inside the knee-length stretch trousers.

Knee pad (C)

Shin pad (O)

Ankle tape (O): joints are heavily strapped for added protection and support.

Boots (C): lightweight studded football boots are best on grass.

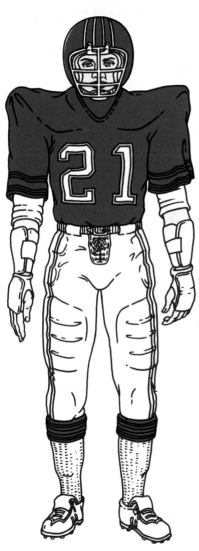

Ready to play! On the outside, the team uniform — jersey, trousers, socks and helmet all in team colours. Jerseys depict a number on the front and back and sometimes on the sleeves as well to identify main playing positions (see below). No two jerseys in a team can have the same number.

Team numbering system

Numbers are used to identify the main playing positions:

1-19 quarterbacks and kickers.

20-49 running backs and defensive backs.

50-59 centres and linebackers.

60-79 defensive and offensive linemen.

80-89 wide receivers and tight ends.

90-99 more defensive linemen and linebackers.

Explanations of the positions are given on pages 12-13 and 18-25.

Hint box: buying equipment

For established teams, equipment may be provided by the club. If you need to buy your own equipment:

● Buy from a reputable specialist shop.

● Or order direct from suppliers (look through the American football magazines for advertisements).

● When buying a helmet, check that it complies with safety requirements (it should have a label with the letters NOCSAE clearly marked).

● Check that your helmet fits snugly without moving about.

THE GAME

Players and Officials

American football is played between two teams of 11 players. At any point in the game, one team has possession of the ball (the offence) and the other is defending (defence). The team with the ball is allowed four attempts or *downs* to advance the ball ten or more yards while the defence tries to prevent this progress. The aim of the game is to get the ball upfield and score (see page 15).

Because unlimited substitution is allowed, most teams have squads of 45-48 players with separate defence, offence and special units. Each player has a specialist position and sometimes a secondary role, but it is very unusual for an offensive specialist to play a defensive position or vice versa.

● As a beginner you should try to play in every possible position before deciding on a speciality.
● Detailed descriptions of the different positions are given on pages 18-25.

Officials

The game is controlled by seven officials who each carry a yellow weighted cloth known as a 'flag' which is thrown to the ground to indicate a foul. Officials all wear black and white striped shirts and white caps — except for the referee, who wears a black cap.

The referee.
The senior official who makes the decision on all calls. He is positioned behind the attacking team. The referee uses a whistle at the start and finish of a play, and a host of signals to indicate what's happening.

The umpire.
Reports infringements behind the defensive *backfield* and records *time outs*.

The head lineman.
Reports on the action at one end of the *line of scrimmage*.

The line judge.
Deals with the other end of the *line of scrimmage* and is also responsible for timing the game.

The back judge.
On the same side of the field as the line judge and reports on pass receptions.

The side judge.
Like the back judge but on the other side of the field.

The field judge.
Covers the plays involving the tight ends (see page 20) and decides if field goals (see page 33) are valid.

The referee signals a *Time Out*.

Offence
(see pages 18-21)

The attacking side — the offence — consists of a centre, two guards, two tackles and two ends to form the offensive line, plus a quarterback and three running backs.

Typical offensive positions:

C   centre
G   guard
T   tackle
TE   tight end
SE/WR   split end/wide receiver
QB   quarterback
RB   running back

These form the offensive line and are known as linemen

Defence
(see pages 22-25)

The defensive team's task is to challenge the offence and try to stop them from making forward progress with the ball. Defensive line-ups can vary according to what the offence are doing — this is discussed in the defensive skills sections on pages 34-35 — but a typical formation prior to the start of a *down* consists of a mix of linemen, linebackers, cornerbacks and safeties as shown here:

DE   defensive end
DT   defensive tackle
LB   linebacker
CB   cornerback
S   safety

| CB | S | S | CB | **Secondary** |

| LB | LB | LB | **Linebackers** |

| DE | DT | DT | DE | **Defensive line** |

Game Overview

The aim of the game

● The ultimate aim is to score more points than your opponents.

● Points are scored when the ball crosses the goal line for a *touchdown* and when it is kicked over the goal crossbar, or run or passed into the endzone (see pages 6-7).

● In order to get the ball upfield to score you have to advance within the framework of the four-down system.

Advancing the ball

The ball can be advanced by:

● **RUSHING** — running with the ball.
● **PASSING** — achieves longer distances but risks interception by the defence.

Four-down system

This is the basis of the game. The offence has four attempts, *downs,* to advance the ball a minimum of ten yards. So when you hear terms like *2nd and 7* this refers to which of the four *downs* the offence is taking (*2nd*) and how many yards they need to advance (*7*). The yards needed and *downs* used are indicated by *down* markers (the *chain gang*).

● If the required yardage — or more — *is* achieved:

the team gets another four *downs.*

● If the required yardage is *not* achieved:
possession of the ball passes to the other team who bring their offence unit onto the field and try to make yardage in the opposite direction.

What if . . . you lose *yardage*?

You have to make up the lost yards in addition to your basic ten. For example, say you are caught in possession 5 yds behind the *line of scrimmage* on your first *down*, you'll have 5 extra yds to make up as well as the original 10. So you'll be *2nd and 15*.

What if . . . your team has used three downs and it seems obvious that you won't make the ten yards?

In this position it's usually best to punt (see pages 25 and 33) the ball deep into the defence's half of the field, especially if you are still in your own half. If you are within 30 or 40 yds of the opponents' goal line, though, it's better to try a field goal (see page 33).

Duration

A game is 60 minutes in total but actually takes much longer because of all the *time out* and stoppages.

First half	Second half
1 Play 15 minutes	**5** Play 15 minutes
2 Change ends	**6** Change ends
3 Play 15 minutes	**7** Play 15 minutes
4 Half time — 20 minute break	

The clock is stopped

- At the end of each play.
- Whenever the ball changes possession.
- When the ball goes out of bounds.
- When a pass is not caught.
- When a team scores.
- When a penalty is awarded.
- Two minutes before half-time and full-time (the two-minute warning).
- Three times in each half by each team at any time they choose.
- For injuries.

Starting

The game starts with a toss of the coin, the winner deciding **either** which team takes the kick-off **or** which end to play. The loser has the choice after half-time.

Kick-off

The kick-off is taken by a special team (see page 24), whose 'place kicker' kicks the ball into the opposition's half.

Kick-off team ready to go . . .

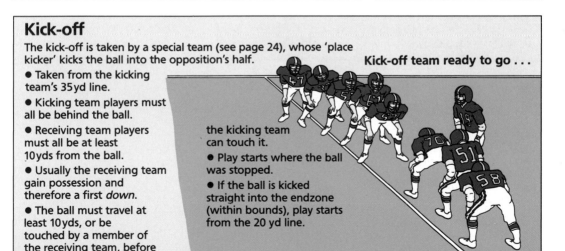

- Taken from the kicking team's 35yd line.
- Kicking team players must all be behind the ball.
- Receiving team players must all be at least 10yds from the ball.
- Usually the receiving team gain possession and therefore a first *down*.
- The ball must travel at least 10yds, or be touched by a member of the receiving team, before the kicking team can touch it.
- Play starts where the ball was stopped.
- If the ball is kicked straight into the endzone (within bounds), play starts from the 20 yd line.

Play

1. The team in possession bring on their offensive unit, the opposing team organise their defence, and they line up along the *line of scrimmage*, with the centre holding the ball.

2. The quarterback, positioned behind the centre, calls instructions to the team (see page 21) and the centre then hands (*snaps*) the ball between his legs to the quarterback. The offence then try to gain yardage.

> **A play STARTS with the *snap* of the ball and ENDS when the ball-carrier is stopped or an attempted pass is incomplete.**

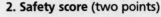

Scoring

Points are scored from:

1. An extra point attempt (one point)

After a successful *touchdown* a kick at the goal is allowed and scores one point if successful. Alternatively, the ball can be run or passed into the endzone, again for one point (NFL rules) or two points (Collegiate and British rules). Both these attempts take place from the three-yard line.

2. Safety score (two points)

This is rather like scoring an own goal in soccer, except that here the opposition can force the error. It occurs when an offensive player is stopped in possession of the ball within his own team's endzone, and results in two points being awarded to the defence.

3. A field goal (three points)

This can be attempted from anywhere on the field and at any time during play. The ball must be kicked from a fixed position or a drop kick (see page 33) and travel through the uprights.

4. A touchdown (six points)

Awarded when a player running with the ball crosses or touches the opponents' goal line, or when a player catches the ball within the opponents' endzone.

Some Rules and Penalties

The British American Football rules run to over 140 pages and it is well worth getting yourself a copy (see page 5). There are many ways in which the rules can be infringed — too many to show here! — and penalties vary according to the severity of the offence.

1 Illegal forward pass

The rule on passing is that only one forward pass is allowed in each scrimmage *down*, and it must be from behind the *line of scrimmage*. You can make as many sideways or backwards passes as you like.

A. Forward pass from other than a scrimmage:
Penalty: 5 yds from where the pass was made.

B. Second pass from behind the line of scrimmage:
Penalty: loss of *down*.

C. Forward pass beyond the line of the scrimmage:
Penalty: loss of *down* and 5 yds.

3 Tripping

Intentional use of the legs to trip an opponent is not allowed at any time.

Penalty: 10 yds.

2 Holding

If you're defending, you can grab an opponent's jersey to grapple him to the ground, but not to stop him running off into open field.

Penalty: 5 yds.

If you're on the offensive side, you must not grab an opponent's jersey at any time.

Penalty: 10 yds.

4 Offside or encroachment

Offensive players must not be in the *neutral zone*, or on the opposition's side of the scrimmage line, before the *snap* of the ball. Defensive players may cross the line but must not have contact with offensive players and must be back in position before the ball is snapped.

Penalty: 5 yds.

On these pages you'll find some of the most common fouls and their penalties — especially those that help explain rules not explained elsewhere — together with the signal given by the referee in each case. Where the penalty given is *yardage*, this means the offence *loses* that distance if the infringement was theirs; and *gains* it if the defence was at fault.

5 Ineligible receiver touches a forward pass

The offensive linemen, the centre, the guards and the tackles, in their normal positions, are not eligible to receive forward passes, or even (intentionally) touch them. In fact, they must not even advance downfield.

Penalty (on or behind the line): loss of *down* at the previous spot (eg *3rd and 5* from your 30 yard line becomes *4th and 5* from the same spot).

(in front of the line): loss of *down* at the previous spot *or* 10 yds.

6 Pass interference

You mustn't interfere with the attempt of an opposing player to catch a forward pass.

Penalty (defence): first *down* awarded to the offence at the point of interference.
(Offence): 10 yds.

7 Delay of game

Once a play is over the next play must start within 30 seconds. Likewise, there must be no overrunning the two-minute *time outs*.

Penalty: 5 yds.

8 Personal foul

Typical personal fouls include *clipping* (blocking below the waist from behind), striking, kicking, piling on and *facemasking*, and all are treated severely.

Penalty (offence): 15 yds.
(defence): 15 yds.
and first *down* to the offence.

Offence

Page 11 showed you a typical offensive formation and identified the players involved. Now for a more detailed look at the offensive unit, and explanations of who does what.

Linemen

● There must be a least seven players on the offensive line. In the example on page 11, these are the centre, two guards, two tackles, a tight end and a split end.

● The centre, guards and tackles constitute the interior line — the heavies whose job is to protect their quarterback from the defence, and undertake *blocking* assignments for running backs.

● For a *passing play* (see pages 36/7) the linemen will try to create time for the quarterback to make a good pass, by creating a *pocket* for him to step into.

● For a *running play* (see pages 38/9) they aim to break a hole in the defensive line to allow their ball-carrier through.

● Interior linemen are not allowed to receive forward passes.

Centre
(C)

Main role

Every play starts from the centre's hands. Usually positioned in the middle of the *line of scrimmage*, you are the one who *snaps* the ball back to your quarterback cleanly. What you do next depends on whether the quarterback has opted for a *passing play* or a *running play* — see above. In either case, your job, with the other interior linemen, is to give the quarterback protection and hold back the defensive linemen.

Skills and attributes
Strength
Speed
Clean *snapping*
Blocking

Guards
(G)

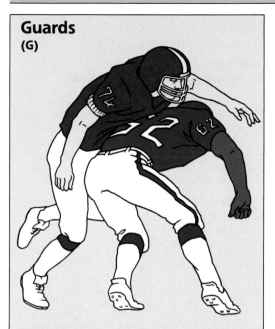

Tackles
(T)

Main role

Guards need to be the fastest of the interior linemen. There are two — a right guard and a left guard, positioned one on each side of the centre. Your job is to protect the ball-carrier and block the opposition. In certain plays you may be required to *pull* the line in one direction to make a *hole* for the ball-carrier to run through.

Main role

Tackles are usually the biggest and strongest of the offensive linemen — you have to be, since your sole responsibility is to stop the opposition getting through your lines.

Skills and attributes
Fitness	*Blocking*
Strength	*Pulling*
Speed	Courage

Skills and attributes
Strength
Courage
Blocking
Pulling

Ends
(TE, SE, WR)

Full backs
(Running backs)
(FB, RB)

Main role

Most offences use a tight end (positioned right next to a tackle) and a split end or wide receiver (positioned apart). Your main function is to run a precise route or running pattern so as to be in the right place at the right time for receiving your quarterback's pass and gaining *yardage*. You need to be versatile when things do not go according to plan!

Main role

One or two will be used according to the selected play. Full backs are running backs used mainly in short *yardage running plays* and usually positioned behind all the other offensive players. You'll often act as a *lead blocker*, making a path for another running back through the line. You are also pass receivers.

Skills and attributes

Speed and size	Running
Versatility	Strength
Catching	*Blocking* (tight ends)

Skills and attributes

Speed and size	Running with the ball
Catching	*Blocking*
Running the pattern	

Halfbacks (Running backs)
(HB, RB, F)

Main role

Speed rather than size is important for a half-back the smaller and faster of the two running backs (also known as a *flanker*). Your main function is to weave skilfully and quickly past the defence and out into the open field ready to receive a pass. You may also act as a *lead blocker.*

Skills and attributes

Speed	Running
Agility	*Blocking*
Catching	

Quarterback
(QB)

Main role

This is the leader of the offence, directing, monitoring and adjusting the offence proceedings. You need to know your play book really well. In the *huddle* between each *down*, you let your players know which play is to follow using an established code system (see page 26). The quarterback is the player who takes the *snap* of the ball from the centre. Depending on the chosen play, you then either *hand off* to a running back, or drop back to pass to a receiver.

Skills and attributes

Excellent memory and quick-thinking brain	Throwing
	Dropping
Leadership qualities	Running

Defence

These pages will tell you more about the roles of the players within the defence unit. Their basic job is to break up the offensive formation and disrupt the proposed plays.

Tackles
(T, NT)

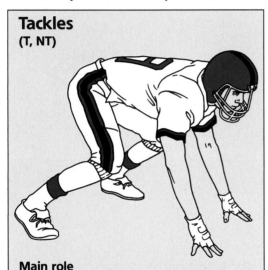

Main role

Your precise role depends on the type of play your opponents are going for. Immediately after the *snap* you must be able to read whether it's a *running play* or *passing play* and act accordingly (see pages 36-9). If there are two of you, you'll usually line up opposite the guards; if there is just one, he's known as a nose tackle and has the hard job of covering the whole area between the guards, including the centre.

Skills and attributes
Size	Tackling
Strength	

Defensive ends
(DE)

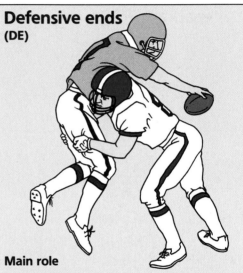

Main role

Your job is not only to stop the offence from getting past the defensive line, but also to fight your way through and on to tackle the quarterback or ball-carrier. You'll need to be fast since you will sometimes have to charge the running back or quarterback from around the end of the line (see page 45).

Skills and attributes
Size	Speed
Strength	Tackling

It's rough work, but there's a lot of satisfaction in getting the ball-carrier onto the ground!
There are many possible defensive formations (see also pages 42-43), each containing a mix of linemen (tackles and ends), linebackers and the secondary (cornerbacks and safeties).

Linebackers
(LB)

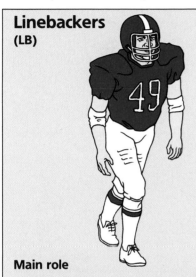

Main role

Positioned behind the linemen, your main task is to get that ball, whether it's in a player's possession or in the air! It could mean going straight in with an attack on the ball-carrier, or backing up the work of a lineman in a tackle or *running play*. And if you can't actually get the ball, at least try to stop the opposition from getting it to the player they're trying to reach.

Skills and attributes
Size	Strength
Speed	Tackling

Secondary
(CB, S)

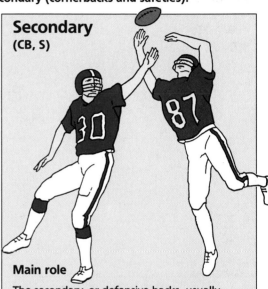

Main role

The secondary, or defensive backs, usually total four and consist of cornerbacks and safeties. You are the second line of defence and it's your job to protect the outer areas against running plays and to stop the ball being passed successfully to the wide receivers.

Skills and attributes
Speed
Tackling

Special Teams

These specialist units are brought onto the field for kick-offs, punts, *extra points* and field goals.

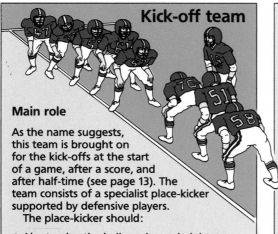

Kick-off team

Main role

As the name suggests, this team is brought on for the kick-offs at the start of a game, after a score, and after half-time (see page 13). The team consists of a specialist place-kicker supported by defensive players.

The place-kicker should:

● Aim to give the ball maximum height, to give his team-mates time to move to tackle the receiver.

● Generally go for as long a kick as possible, though if your side is losing, it's sometimes worth kicking the ball along the ground for the minimum 10 yds, hoping that your own team will get possession (an *onside kick*). The rest of the unit:

● Line up, five on each side of the kicker.

● When the kick has been made, run at top speed to tackle the returner downfield.

Skills and attributes
Cool head and strong nerves
Kicking skills

Kick-off return team

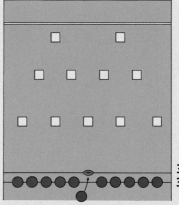

35 yd line
30 yd line

Main role

These are the players on the receiving team. Your main job here is to protect the receiver if he's made a good catch, and to block tackles so the receiver can gain as much *yardage* as possible.

If the receiver anticipates trouble from the tackles before making the catch, he can call for a *fair catch*. This gives automatic protection from tackles but he must not move on with the ball, and the next *down* starts from where the catch was made.

Skills and attributes
Receiver: catching   running
Others: *blocking*

Punting team

Main role

If, after a third *down*, your team has little chance of making the required *yardage*, the special punting team is likely to be brought on. This unit consists of a punter with linemen to protect him. The idea is to send the ball deep into your opponents' half so that their offensive play starts as far as possible from your goal. To make a punt, the ball is *snapped* to the kicker from the scrimmage. He then drops the ball and kicks it before it hits the ground.

Skills and attributes
Cool head and strong nerves
Kicking/punting skills

Punt return team

Main role

The main task here is to protect your punt returner from being tackled by the opposition, who will be heading his way as soon as the ball is *snapped*. The punt returner himself is in the unenviable position of waiting to catch the ball while the opposition rush towards him ready to tackle. Like the kick-off receiver, he can opt for a *fair catch*.

45 yds

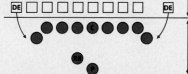

Skills and attributes
Punt returner: catching, running, strong nerves
Others: *blocking*

Field goal unit

Main role

When your team is within range of your opponents' goal, and usually on a fourth *down*, the field goal unit will come into play. This consists of the centre, a holder (sometimes the quarterback) and a kicker as well as the offensive line. The holder receives the *snap* and places the ball on the ground directly in front of the goal posts, and the kicker then tries to send it over the bar for three points.

7 yds

Skills and attributes
Kicking

BASIC SKILLS AND STANCES

This section shows you some of the basic skills and stances needed, both for the offensive and defensive games. Practise them often with your team-mates.

Offensive Skills

The base

This is a basic two-point stance.

Used by: mainly linebackers and defensive ends; sometimes running backs.

Purpose: to give you stability immediately before contact with an opponent.

- Feet are shoulder width apart, facing forwards and parallel to each other.

- Squat down to a crouch position.

- Keep your back straight.

- Keep your head up.

Three-point stance

An extension of the *base stance*. From this stance you can go in any direction.

Used by: all offensive line players and running backs.

Purpose: to give you the best start to a play.

- From a base position, move your right foot (left if you're left-footed) back a few inches.

- Lean forwards and put your right hand on the ground in front of your right knee.

- Get your shoulders parallel to the ground.

- Keep your head up.

- Make sure your hand is not too far forward — you should be able to lift your hand without toppling over.

The snap

Used by: centre (*snaps* the ball to quarterback).

Purpose: to start a *down*.

Centre
● Adopt three-point stance, holding the ball in either hand.
● The laces on the ball should be to the left.
● Charge forward as you snap the ball — or hold your ground for a *pass play*.

Quarterback
● Bend knees with feet shoulder width.
● Spread your hands, with thumbs touching, between centre's legs.
● Keep your back straight and head up — watch the defence.
● When the ball is *snapped*, pull it in to your stomach.

The hand off

Used by: quarterback (hands off to running back)

Purpose: to transfer the ball in a *running play*

Running back
● Make a *pocket* to receive the ball with your arms as shown.
● Once you've got the ball securely, tuck it away under your arm with your fingers over the end.

Quarterback
● Before the *hand off*, keep your eyes on the runner's stomach and place the ball there firmly.
● Keep the whole action smooth.

The drop

Used by: quarterback.

Purpose: to move back quickly and smoothly from the *line of scrimmage* on a *passing play* (see page 36). A *drop* can be of three steps (for short passes), five steps (for medium length throws) or seven steps (for *bombs*).

● After taking the *snap*, you must sprint as fast as you can to your passing position.
● Take a long first step, turning your body so you're at right angles to the *line of scrimmage* as you do so.
● Complete your turn on your second long step, so you've got your back to the line.
● Run your remaining steps like this but look over your shoulder so you can see downfield.
● When you get to your passing position, keep your legs moving while you find your target: then throw.

The pass

Used by: quarterback

Purpose: to send the ball to the running back in a *passing* play.
When you're in your pass position and can see your target receiver:

● Grip the ball firmly over the laces, with spread fingers and both hands.
● Hold the ball on your chest.
● Step towards your target and keep your eyes on him.
● Whip round as you release the ball.
● Follow through with your arm and body.

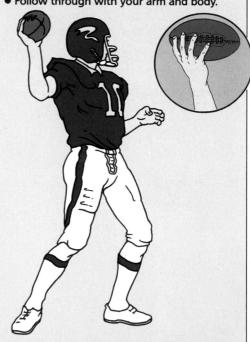

Catching

Used by: pass receivers.

Purpose: to catch the ball cleanly when it is passed to you.

● To catch the ball, you first have to run into the pre-planned position, using one of many practised routes — see Running the pattern (page 32).
● Whatever route you are running, try to be as fast and accurate as possible.
● Once you are in position, adopt an upright stance with your outside foot forwards, then turn to watch the ball.
● Keep your eye on the ball all the time.
● Don't wait for a high pass to come to you — jump for it.
● Catch it in your hands, away from your body and with spread fingers, not against your chest.
● Then quickly bring the ball in to your body and tuck it safely under your arm.

Catching practice

You can improve your catching skills with these simple drills:

1. Stand about 5ft apart, feet shoulder width, back straight.
● Now throw the ball fast to each other.
● With each catch, lock the ball in to your body and throw it straight back without a pause.
● Throw to different positions.

2. As before, but this time kneel on the ground. When you have to lean out to catch the ball, pull it in to your body immediately, then roll, keeping your arm underneath you to avoid hurting your shoulder.

3. Stand in a base stance 5ft away from your team-mate and facing away from him. As he throws you the ball he shouts BALL and you then whirl around to take the catch.

Blocking

The quarterback and running backs may get all the glory but they wouldn't achieve anything without good *blocking* from their linemen!

Used by: offensive linemen, receivers and runners.

Purpose: to stop defenders from getting to the ball carrier; to cut them off from your *backfield*; to guard your running back by staying in front of him to fend off any tackles (*lead blocking*).

There are numerous variations using head, shoulders, body and arms, and some techniques use more than one player. Here are some of the most common.

1 Drive block

An effective way of moving your opponent out of the way of the running back.

● Step towards your opponent on your right foot.
● Look at his chin.
● Get your facemask into the numbers of his shirt.
● Drive your hands into his armpits.
● Keep pushing up through him hard.
● Keep your feet firm, shoulder width apart, and your stance low.
● Don't stop or he'll charge again!

2 Cut block

Useful for delaying or diverting your opponent as he tries to reach the action.

● Initial contact is similar to a drive block.
● Then drop into a crawling position, turning as you do so.
● He should trip over you — but be careful not to drop too soon or he'll just throw you out of the way instead!

3 Pass block

Probably the hardest blocking technique to master, but very effective if you can get it right. Pass blocking entails striking repeatedly at your opponent: think of it as a sequence: set-hit-recoil.

● SET: move to a base position.
● HIT: extend your arms and use the heels of your hands, keep your elbows in and drive him off, using your legs as a power base. Keep your feet moving.
● RECOIL: back off into your *base stance* and wait for his next charge.
● You must stay between the defender and your quarterback — and that's the tricky bit.

What can't you do?

Blocking is rough, but there are some rules.
● You mustn't use your hands to hold or grab your opponent.
● You mustn't encircle him with your arms.
● You mustn't go for his neck or head.
● You must only block from the front.
The penalty for illegal use of hands is ten yards.

Pulling

In some plays linemen are required to *pull*, or come off the *line of scrimmage*; it needs to be done quickly and smoothly.

Used by: all linemen.

Purpose: to lead a play around the end of the line, or to trap a particular defensive lineman.

To pull out to the right:
● Stick your right elbow into your waist and whip your arm round to the right.
● Step to the right with your right foot.
● Sprint along the *line of scrimmage*.
● Run straight.

Running with the ball

Used by: running backs, ends, quarterbacks.

Purpose: to keep possession and gain yardage.

● If you've got a *lead blocker*, follow him closely — his job is to protect you!
● When threatened by a defender, try a change of pace or direction; stop and start, side-step or use any other trick you can.
● When you have to, strike a defender with your outstretched free arm: hit him hard, then use your arm to push off and away from him.
● As a last resort, hug the ball tight in both arms, get into base position and block. Keep your head up.

Running the pattern

By using pre-planned routes, the quarterback knows where you will be. There is an infinite number of possible routes.

Used by: runners.

Purpose: to get into the pre-planned position to take the pass.

● Make sure you know your plays and routes inside out.
● Run fast and low, with your body leaning forward.
● Keep as true to the route as you can.
● When you meet a defender, run straight at him without breaking your stride.
● As you approach him, take a hard *feint step* at him, then *cut* in the opposite direction.

The Punt

Goal kicks

Used by: specialist punter in punt unit.

Purpose: to send the ball as far into your opponent's territory as possible on a fourth *down* if you cannot make your required *yardage*.

● Position yourself 12-15 yds behind the *line of scrimmage*.
● Get right behind the ball to catch it from the *snap*.
● Step onto your kicking foot, then onto the other and drop the ball.
● Kick the ball before it hits the ground, aiming to make contact with its bottom half for added height.
● Follow through until your foot is level with your hand.

The technique is the same for goal kicks after a *touchdown* and field goal kicks.

Used by: goal-kicking special unit.

Purpose: to score!

● You can kick straight at the goal or from an angle.
● Make sure your non-kicking foot is pointing at the goal post.
● You'll get more height if your non-kicking foot is further back.
● Keep your eye on the ball and follow through.

Defensive Skills

Four-point stance

Because the initial movement of a defensive lineman is a forward surge, a four-point stance is sometimes adopted in preference to the three-point stance.
It gives you good forward momentum.

Used by: defensive linemen.

Purpose: to give you optimum acceleration at the start of a play.

● From a base position, drop one foot back a little.
● Lean forwards with both hands on the ground, right under your shoulders.
● Keep your back level with the ground — and look up.

Tackling

Used by: all defensive players.

Purpose: to stop the ball-carrier and gain possession.

● You can only tackle the ball-carrier.
● Tackling is more about determination than skill — just charge in there and stop him!
● As you approach, keep your eyes open and fixed on his stomach.
● You can use your hands and arms to encircle, grab, pull, push or knock him to the ground.
● Try to get your head in front of him.
● If a team-mate is already tackling the ball-carrier, you can go straight for the ball.
● For a tackle from the side, get your head in front of your opponent.

The jam and the shed

A jam is getting a good hold of your opponent — then you shed him to one side.

Used by: defensive linemen and linebackers.

Purpose: to get past blockers to the ball-carrier.
● Run past a blocker if you possibly can.

If you have to take him on:
● Adopt the base position.
● Hit upwards through his shoulder pads or get your shoulder in his belt and push hard with your arms.
● Feel which way he's trying to move you, and resist.
● Remember that his job is to get you away from the ball-carrier — so if you're being pushed to the right, the action will be on the left.
● If you can shed him in the same direction he's trying to move you, the ball-carrier should run straight into you!

The swim

Used by: defensive linemen

Purpose: a useful technique for getting past an offensive lineman. It must be done in one fast smooth movement.

● Grab him by the shoulder pads and push him back.
● As he comes back to you, pull him sideways towards you.
● Then step forward with your inside foot and swing your inside arm over his head (this looks like a swimming stroke, hence the name).
● Try to push him back with your elbow as you complete the movement.

OFFENSIVE PLAY

Offensive play is all about action — and the action revolves around either a *passing play* or a *running play.*

Which play?

● Your team will have hundreds of different plays rehearsed, each with a different code known only to your side.
● In the huddle preceding each *down*, your quarterback explains the next play.
● You then take up your positions and the quarterback counts into the play.

What if . . . the quarterback needs to change the plan at the last minute?

He might do this if the defence are lining up in a way which would upset the planned play. He lets you know on the *line of scrimmage* by including the new play in his countdown — this is called an audible.

Passing Play
Drop back pass

It sounds simple — but a drop-back pass is easy for the defence to read and they will be hard to keep at bay.

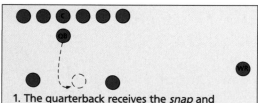

1. The quarterback receives the *snap* and *drops* back before turning to throw (see *The drop*, page 28).

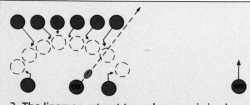

2. The linemen retreat to make a semi-circular *pocket* to surround the quarterback.

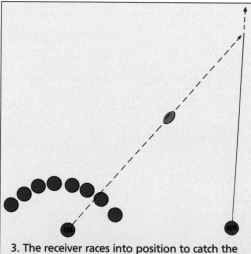

3. The receiver races into position to catch the ball from the quarterback and gain as much *yardage* as possible.

Play action

This is designed to confuse the defence because it pretends to be a *running play* but develops into a passing play. If you're lucky it gives you about a second's headstart before the defence realises what you are doing.

1. The quarterback turns as if he's making a *handoff* to the running back.
2. The running back pretends to take the ball and runs downfield.
3. The quarterback then passes to one of the receivers.

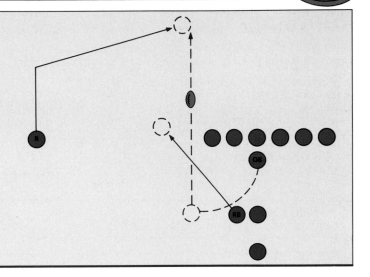

Screen pass

This is another way of trying to fool the defence. Again, it may buy you a little time, but the defence will soon see what you're up to!

1. The linemen retreat to make a *pocket* as for a drop back pass.
2. The quarterback pumps his arm as if to make a long pass.
3. Instead he makes a short pass to a running back who has moved laterally towards the sideline.
4. Two or more linemen join the runner as *lead blockers*.

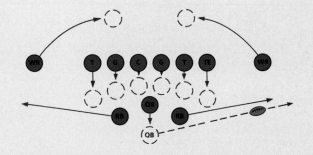

Running Plays

Every good team will have a large repertoire of running plays, some highly complex. These are some of the most basic and should be practised regularly.

The sweep

This is a wide play which uses *lead blockers*.

1. The quarterback pitches the ball laterally to his receiver.
2. The ball-carrier follows the *lead blockers* around the outside of the line.

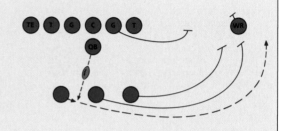

The draw

Another tactic to confuse the defence — this one is a run that looks like a pass. Usually used for *short yardage situations*.

1. At the *snap* , the quarterback drops back three paces and the linemen withdraw to form a *pocket*.
2. Instead of passing, the quarterback discreetly *hands off* to the full back.
3. The full back then blasts through the *line of scrimmage*.

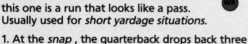

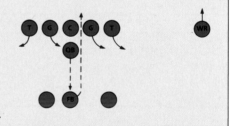

The dive

This is a quick running play, one of the most basic in any team's repertoire.

1. After a short *snap* count, the quarterback moves quickly to the left or right and *hands off* to the running back.
2. The offensive linemen charge forward to knock back the defence and the runner follows to gain as many yards as possible.

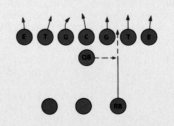

The trap

There are many variations on the trap, but the idea is to deceive a defensive lineman and create a hole in the defence for the runner to get through.

1. Here the left guard moves to one side rather than *blocking* the defensive tackle.
2. The tackle moves to fill the gap but is hit from the side by the centre.
3. The quarterback has handed off the ball to the running back who now charges through the hole in the line.

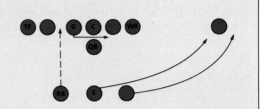

The quarterback sneak

Useful for *short yardage* plays.

1. The quarterback receives the ball from the centre and retains it.
2. He then rushes forward, either directly behind, or to the right or left of, the centre.
3. The centre acts as *lead blocker*.

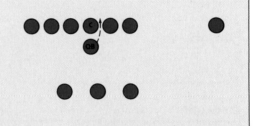

The bootleg

If you've been running sweep plays, the *bootleg* will confuse the defence because it looks like the same thing. Useful for *short yardage* plays but with high risk of injury to the quarterback if it fails.

1. The quarterback fakes a *pitch* to the running back.
2. He actually retains the ball himself, concealing it on his hip and upper thigh.
3. He then sprints to the opposite side from the sweep action.

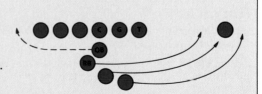

Offensive Line Formations

The way the players line up at the start of a play will vary according to the wishes of the coach and the strengths and weaknesses of the team. There are numerous variations, but this page highlights the most commonly used.

Pro set

This is the most common offensive line-up you'll see on televised games.

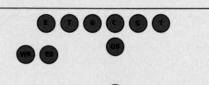

T formation

Probably the easiest for beginners. Often used for running plays where the running back is going round the outside of the line. There are many variations: a common one is to replace the tight end with a split end.

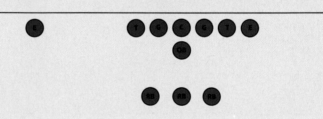

I formation

Good for running plays with lots of protection in front of the running back to give him time to make *yardage*.

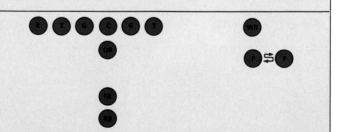

Shotgun

A popular formation for *passing plays*, this one has the quarterback well back from the line.

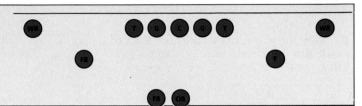

Short yardage formation

This is what it sounds like: a useful line-up when you're nearly at the goal line, or for a first *down*.

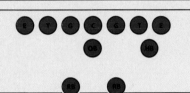

Wishbone

This formation gives the quarterback a choice: to run with the ball himself, protected by a half back, or to hand the ball to the full back, or to throw the ball out to the other half back. After the *snap*, he can wait a split second to see where the defensive linebacker goes before making his choice.

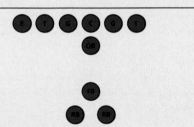

What if . . . the offensive line doesn't hold?

If there is no way of continuing the proposed play, the quarterback will have to *scramble* to avoid being *sacked*. This means dodging around, ultimately to the safety of the sidelines if the receivers can't find a spot where they can take a pass. Meanwhile, receivers should forget their rehearsed routes and do anything they can to make themselves accessible and visible to the quarterback.

DEFENSIVE PLAY

If offence is all about action, defence is about reaction. The aim of the defence is to ward off the offensive line and get as many men to the ball-carrier, as fast as possible.

The huddle

Before each play, the defence will huddle in the same way as the offence, with one player acting as captain and telling you what your assignment will be on the next down.

Zones

Successful defence means having all the offensive players covered. One effective way of doing this is to imagine the area behind the *line of scrimmage* divided into zones. See page 45.

Defensive formations

There are just as many line-ups possible on the defence as there are on the offence. Before the *snap*, defensive players are not restricted in their movements, and last minute changes are often made to confuse the offence. Here are some of the most common starting line-ups.

5-3

This means there are five linemen, three linebackers and three secondaries. This is a useful formation for both the *passing play* and *running play*.

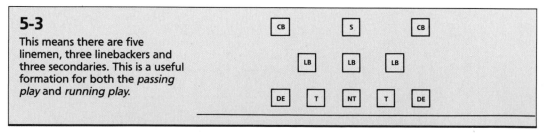

6-3

This formation has everyone up front, so it is only used in a *short yardage situation* where a long pass is unlikely.

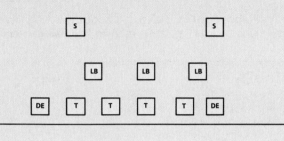

4-3

This is useful if you are expecting a *passing play*, because there are four men in the front to rush the quarterback, and several *secondary* players to cover the receivers.

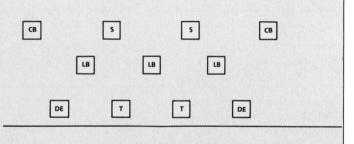

5-2

Here there are three linemen, but the two outside linebackers are up on the line as well. It is a useful all-purpose formation because you have four men in the *secondary* to cover a pass, and the linebackers can be ready to react to either a *passing* or *running play*. The only disadvantage is that the nose tackle is on his own between the guards.

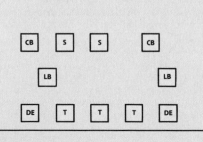

Defence Against Running Play

You'll recognise a *running play* when the offensive linemen come forward to *block* rather than drop back to make a *pocket*. But be careful that they're not faking! The rule is: don't commit yourself until you know what the play is. Then move like lightning to stop the run. You need to work as a team, and everyone has a role to play.

Defensive linemen

Your job is to stand your ground against the oncoming offensive linemen, resist being moved to one side, and stop them creating a gap. Which of the linemen you are asked to key depends on the play and formation: this diagram shows a slant play for four linemen.

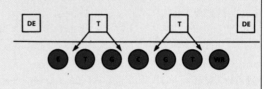

Linebackers

Since your linemen are outnumbered, you must back them up on a running play. Plug any gaps in your own line, or get through to the ball-carrier if you see a weak spot in the offensive line. Sometimes you may be asked to *blitz* on a *running play* — just forget your usual duties and charge the quarterback. On a stack play, shown here, a linebacker positions himself directly behind a lineman, giving the offensive linemen the problem of guessing which way he's going to go.

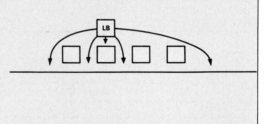

Cornerbacks and safeties

Your main responsibility is to deal with the receivers on *passing plays* — but that doesn't mean you can stand around at the back on *running plays*! Keep your eye on the guard and tackle on your side and move in only when you are sure it's a running play.

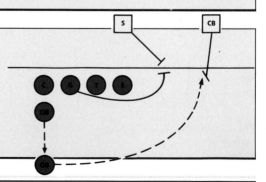

Defence Against Passing Play

For a pass, the offensive linemen drop back to make a *pocket* for the quarterback — but again, be on guard for fakes before you commit yourselves to responding. On a *passing play* there are five possible receivers scattering in the backfield. One will be the quarterback's first target, a second will be on standby, and the others will act as decoys.

Of course, you won't immediately know which is which.

Linemen: it is your job to get to the quarterback and stop him before he gets into position and makes the pass.	**Linebackers:** you are responsible for defending against short passes in the middle area, but for any other *passing play*, go in and support the linemen.

Cornerbacks and safeties: you hold the most vital role in *passing play* defence, and must cover all the possible receivers. You have a choice of action:

Man-for-man

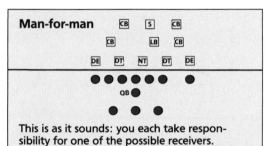

This is as it sounds: you each take responsibility for one of the possible receivers.

Zone defence

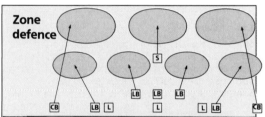

A safer option than man-to-man defence, here you each cover an area of the field.

Blitz

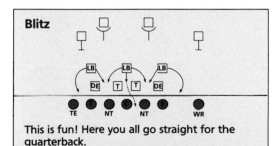

This is fun! Here you all go straight for the quarterback.

What if . . . you don't stop the pass being made?

Once the quarterback has actually thrown the ball, you will know which receiver it's aimed at. Rush straight to him and try to intercept the pass or, failing that, knock it away from him. If he's already caught it, you can tackle — but make sure you don't do it too early or you'll be penalised for pass interference.

Warm-Up

Warming up with gentle stretching exercises is *vital* before a full-length game — and recommended as preparation even before a practice session. If you play without stretching your muscles first, you are likely to suffer injuries as a result. Here are some basic stretches — your warm-up should be at least ten minutes long.

IMPORTANT: Minor injuries are inevitable with any contact sport. If there is no improvement after 48 hours, or if in doubt, always seek medical advice.

1 Shoulder and upper back stretch

Put your hands behind your head and press your shoulders and elbows backwards. Stretch and hold for 15 seconds. Repeat ten times.

2 Calf and thigh stretches

Kick your legs up behind you, as high as you can — ten each side. Do the same again, this time holding your foot as shown for a count of 15.

3 Groin and hamstring stretches

Stretch one leg out to the side, with the other bent as shown and hold for the count of five — three each side.

4 Back and stomach stretches

Bending from the hips, touch your right foot with your left hand, then straighten up and repeat on the other side — ten each side.

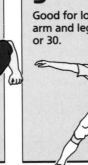

5 Star jumps

Good for loosening your arm and leg joints — do 25 or 30.

6 Jogging and sprinting

Run around the pitch at a jogging pace, interspersed with short sprints.

Hints for Improving Your Game

Offence

Know your plays

● Make sure you really know the codes and what each play means to you: and stick to your specific task as closely as you can without watching what the next man is doing. Remember, if every man does his job exactly right, the play will succeed.

● On first *down* — go for a touchdown.

● On third *down* — don't take risks: concentrate on making your *yardage* and retaining the ball for another first *down*.

● Don't gamble unless you are well ahead or are about to lose!

● If you find a successful formula — stick with it.

Defence

● Be ready for anything: you have to adapt fast to what the offence is doing.

● Don't gamble if you're in front.

● Try to aniticipate — what would *you* do if you were their quarterback?

● Learn to read the plays quickly.

● Are the offensive linemen backing off to make a *pocket*? Expect a *passing play.*

● Does one of the backs look nervous? It could be his turn to take the pass.

● Do the linemen surge forward straight away? It's a *running play* this time.

● Always be on the watch for fakes!

Glossary

This glossary explains terms encountered in the text as well as some others you may hear whilst playing or watching a game.

BASE STANCE   Basic crouched position used especially by linebackers.

BACKFIELD   Dual term: either a collective name for the quarterback and running backs or the area where they start, behind the offence's line of scrimmage.

BLITZ   A spectacular assault on the quarterback by the defensive linebackers and safeties.

BLOCK   A legal obstruction to prevent a defender from reaching the ball-carrier.

BOMB   A very long pass, often thrown as a last resort.

BOOTLEG   A fake play where the quarterback pretends to hand off to a running back and then conceals the ball and runs with it himself.

CHAIN GANG (OR CHAIN CREW)   The sideline officials who indicate the yardage gained and required, using a ten yard measuring chain.

CLIPPING   A dangerous and illegal block made from the side or behind.

COMPLETION   To catch a forward pass successfully.

CUT   To change direction suddenly while running at speed.

DEAD BALL   Any ball that is out of play.

DOWN   A play from the line of scrimmage; the offence has four downs to gain ten yards.

DROP   The action of the quarterback moving back from the line of scrimmage to set up a pass.

EXTRA POINT   Awarded after a touchdown if the place kicker successfully kicks the ball through the goal uprights over the crossbar.

FACEMASKING   When a defensive/offensive player tackles the ball-carrier by his mask. Very dangerous and illegal.

FAIR CATCH   When the catcher of a kicked ball indicates by raising his arm that he is going to catch the ball without running on: he is then protected from interference from defenders.

FALSE START   Where an offensive player moves before the snap of the ball once the line is set: this is illegal and the penalty is loss of five yards.

FEINT STEP   Pretending to go one way, when actually you are going another.

...ame for a wide ... split running

...all-carrier fumbles if he drops the ball, either accidentally or as a result of a tackle. The ball is still in play and up for grabs by a player from either side.

GAME PLAN The strategic plan of plays and formations a coach organises for each game.

HANDOFF The action of the quarterback handing the ball to a running back.

HANG TIME The time a punt or kick stays in the air.

HOLE A gap in the defence created by offensive linemen for the ball-carrier to run through.

HUDDLE The get-together between plays where the quarterback gives his team instructions; defence teams also use the huddle to plan their strategies.

INCOMPLETE PASS (OR INCOMPLE-TION) A pass that is neither caught nor intercepted. This may be a deliberate ploy on the part of the quarterback when, to avoid being sacked, he deliberately under- or over-throws a pass — but he must be careful not to be caught on an intentional grounding fault.

INTENTIONAL GROUNDING A pass that the quarterback deliberately throws on the ground to avoid being sacked. This is illegal and heavily penalised.

LATERAL PASS A sideway or backwards pass.

LEAD BLOCKER An offensive player forging ahead of a runner to protect him from being tackled by the defence.

LINE OF SCRIMMAGE The imaginary line passing through the top of the ball, on either side of which the teams line up prior to the snap of the ball.

NCAA National Collegiate Athletic Association.

NEUTRAL ZONE An 11 inch (the length of the football) strip of ground running across the width of the pitch, into which no player may go before the snap of the ball.

NFL National Football League.

OFFSIDE A lineman who goes across the line of scrimmage before the snap is offside.

ONSIDE KICK A short kick from the kick-off used if a team is desperate to regain possession. It must travel the minimum 10 yards.

PASSING PLAY A play where the quarterback passes the ball to a running back.

PITCH/ PITCHOUT An underarm throw of the ball from quarterback to runner.

PLAY ACTION A passing play that starts off looking like a running play.

POCKET The area created by offensive linemen to protect the quarterback while he sets up to pass.

PULL For an offensive lineman to leave the line of scrimmage and act as a lead block for a runner.

RETURN The amount of distance in yards made by a player who collects a kick or intercepts a pass.

RUNNING PLAY A play where the quarterback hands off the ball to a runner, or pitches it, or runs with it himself.

SACK To tackle the quarterback when he has the ball behind the line of scrimmage.

SAFETY POINTS A score of two points to the defence when the ball-carrier is caught in possession of the ball in his own endzone.

SCRAMBLE The dodging around of a quarterback when his offensive play has collapsed and he is trying to avoid being sacked.

SCREEN PASS A passing play that starts off looking like a running play.

SECONDARY Collective name for cornerbacks and safeties.

SET When the linemen take up their three-point stance or established alignment just before the snap of the ball. Once the line is *set* they may not move before the snap.

SHORT YARDAGE SITUATION When the offence is close to making the first down.

SNAP The action of passing the ball through the centre's legs to the quarterback at the start of each play.

STRAIGHT-ARM To fend off a tackler by stretching out your arm and hitting him with your palm.

STRONG SIDE The side of the offensive formation where the tight end is positioned.

TIME OUT When the game clock is stopped, either by an official putting a flag on the play or at the request of one of the teams.

TOUCHDOWN The scoring of six points when a player crosses the opposition's goal line with the ball (it needn't be grounded) or takes a pass in the endzone.

WEAK SIDE The side of the offensive formation without a tight end.

YARDAGE The distance a team gains, measured in yards.

Printed in Italy